Growing Up in
Germany

Other titles in the *Growing Up Around the World* series include:

Growing Up in
Germany

Barbara Sheen

ReferencePoint
Press®

San Diego, CA

© 2018 ReferencePoint Press, Inc.
Printed in the United States

For more information, contact:
ReferencePoint Press, Inc.
PO Box 27779
San Diego, CA 92198
www.ReferencePointPress.com

LIBRARY OF CONGRESS CATALOGING-IN-PUBLICATION DATA

Name: Sheen, Barbara, author.
Title: Growing Up in Germany/by Barbara Sheen.
Description: San Diego, CA: ReferencePoint Press, 2018. | Series: Growing Up
   Around the World series | Includes bibliographical references and index.
Identifiers: LCCN 2017023862 (print) | ISBN
   9781682822111 (hardback) | ISBN 9781682822128 (eBook)
Subjects: LCSH: Germany—Social life and customs—Juvenile literature. |
   Adolescence—Germany—Juvenile literature. | Children—Germany—Juvenile
   literature. | Families—Germany—Juvenile literature. |
Education—Germany—Juvenile literature

CONTENTS

Official Name
Federal Republic
of Germany

Capital ●
Berlin

Size
137,846 square miles
(357,020 sq. km)

Total Population
80,722,792 as of 2016

Youth Population ●
0–14 years: 12.83%
15–24 years: 10.22%

Religion ●
Protestant: 34%;
Catholic: 34%;
Muslim: 3.7%;
unspecified: 28%

Type of Government
Federal parliamentary republic

Language
German

Currency
Euro

Industries
Iron, steel, motor vehicles,
chemicals, machinery,
electronics, shipbuilding,
textiles

Literacy ●
99% (age 15+ able to
read and write)

Internet Users
70.82 million, or 87.6% of
the population as of 2015

CHAPTER ONE

A Progressive and Prosperous Nation

When people think of Germany, they often think of storybook castles, snowcapped mountains, classical music, raucous beer fests, and verdant forests. But there is a lot more to this complicated nation. Germany is home to modern cities, thriving industries, world-famous universities, hardworking people, and a growing multiethnic population. It has a generous social welfare system, a key leadership role in the European Union (EU), and the fifth-largest economy in the world. It also has a conflicted history that includes two devastating world wars, the Holocaust, and the rise and fall of the Berlin Wall.

Yet despite its defeats in World Wars I and II and its post–World War II division into East and West Germany, today's reunified Germany has successfully remade itself into a peaceful, forward-thinking nation. Young people growing up in Germany live in one of the most progressive and prosperous countries on Earth. Their world is one of freedom and opportunity. As an article on the *Travel Blog,* an online world travel diary, explains, "Despite, or perhaps because of its dark recent history, Germany has developed into a tolerant nation seeking compromise rather than confrontation. These days it is a place people run to, rather than run from."[1]

Geography

Germany is a large, geographically diverse nation located in the heart of central Europe. It is bordered by Poland and the Czech Republic to the east; Austria and Switzerland to the south; France, Belgium, the Netherlands, and Luxembourg to the west; and Denmark and the North and Baltic Seas to the north. Covering an area of 137,846 square miles (357,020 sq. km), it is a little smaller than the US state of Montana, and it is the seventh-largest country in Europe.

Germany's terrain includes flat plains, rolling hills, and towering mountains that contain some of Europe's highest peaks. It also has hundreds of lakes as well as great rivers that carry large ships hauling industrial freight to the nation's major seaports. Almost one-third of the country is made up of dense evergreen forests that supply both wood for Germany's flourishing timber industry and natural green areas where Germans hike, camp, and picnic.

Unspoiled meadows filled with wildflowers are a common sight, as are fertile farmlands. Dairy farms, along with farms that produce potatoes, cabbage, wheat, beets, and grapes, among

"Despite, or perhaps because of its dark recent history, Germany has developed into a tolerant nation seeking compromise rather than confrontation. These days it is a place people run to, rather than run from."[1]

—*Travel Blog*, an online travel diary

One of central Europe's most important waterways, the Elbe River (pictured) winds its way through northern Germany. Wetlands teeming with wildlife and picturesque vineyards and villages dot the landscape.

other crops, thrive here. Eifel Mausi, an American who lives in Germany with her German husband, describes the landscape as "stunning. . . . It's one of the greenest areas you'll ever see. Forests, rolling hills, mountains, volcanic lakes, flowers."[2]

Germany's annual rainfall, which ranges from 23 to 48 inches (58 to 122 cm), contributes to its lushness. The climate varies depending on the region. In general, the summers are warm and pleasant, and the winters are cold, gray, and damp. According to author Peter Wortsman, "Wintry Berlin is a city largely devoid of color except for a dirty white carpet of snow flung over a treacherous ice slick and a perennial gray cloud overhead."[3]

A Conflicted History

Germany is a relatively young nation. Although the area that makes up modern Germany has been inhabited for more than two thousand years, for most of its history it has not been unified. Instead, it consisted of warring nation-states ruled by local princes and other noblemen. During the eighth century much of central Europe, including these nation-states, was conquered by Charlemagne and later was part of the Holy Roman Empire.

When the empire collapsed in 1806, Germany remained a hodgepodge of kingdoms. In 1871, however, a statesman named Otto von Bismarck unified the nation and became its first chancellor. The new nation soon became involved in political tensions with some of its neighbors and formed alliances with others. In 1914 the assassination of an Austrian archduke triggered an international crisis that led to World War I. Germany, in alliance with Austria-Hungary and the Ottoman Empire, fought against France, Russia, Great Britain, and eventually the United States. The war lasted four years and was one of the most brutal conflicts in history. More than 9 million soldiers and 7 million civilians were killed. After the war, the victors punished Germany and its allies for the devastation the war had caused. Germany was forced to reduce its armed forces, shut down many of its industries, and pay the equivalent of $31.5 billion in reparations. To finance the reparations, the German government printed huge amounts of money, which led to hyperinflation, devalued currency, and massive unemployment. At the time it was common to see German housewives pushing wheelbarrows full of devalued money to markets just to buy food.

By the 1920s a politician named Adolf Hitler was rising to power. As the leader of the National Socialist (Nazi) Party, Hitler promised to rebuild Germany's army, fix the economy, and create jobs. He blamed Germany's problems on the nation's population of Jews, whom he considered to be an inferior race. In 1933 Hitler was elected Germany's chancellor. A man named Jared, who was a child at the time, recalls that "Hitler promised people work, so they voted for him."[4]

Under Hitler's rule, more jobs were indeed created, and Germany's military was strengthened. In 1939, in an effort to conquer the continent, Germany invaded Poland. This led to the start of

Becoming a German Citizen

The path to citizenship for Germany's immigrant and refugee population is not a simple one. Individuals must be legal residents of Germany for at least eight years before applying for citizenship. They must also meet other requirements. With the exception of young people under the age of twenty-three, applicants must prove that they are gainfully employed and can support themselves and their dependents. They must have a command of the German language. They must take an oath to support the German constitution, and they must give up their former citizenship.

Foreign spouses of German citizens, on the other hand, do not have to live in Germany for eight years before they can apply for citizenship. These individuals must be married to a German for at least two years and have lived in Germany for at least three.

Other rules apply for non-German babies born in Germany. A baby is a citizen at birth if at least one of its parents is a citizen. If neither parent is a citizen, a child can be a citizen from birth only if one of its parents has a permanent residence permit and has lived legally in Germany for a minimum of eight years. About one hundred thousand non-German babies are born in Germany annually.

World War II. Within a short time, Germany had invaded and controlled great swathes of Europe. Before Germany was defeated in 1945, almost every country in the world became involved in the war, with the four major Allies—Great Britain, France, the Soviet Union, and the United States—leading the fight against the main Axis powers of Germany, Italy, and Japan.

While the war raged, the Nazis rounded up Jews, disabled individuals, homosexuals, gypsies, and other people they deemed inferior, imprisoning them in concentration camps where they were worked to death, tortured, and/or deliberately killed. An estimated 9 million people were murdered in the camps, including 6 million Jews. The mass murder of these 6 million Jews is known as the Holocaust. And although contemporary German young-

Deported Jews arrive by train at Auschwitz-Birkenau in Poland, the largest of the Nazi concentration camps. Germany's Nazis systematically killed millions of Jews during World War II, an event that came to be known as the Holocaust.

sters had nothing to do with the atrocities, the Holocaust serves as a historical burden that many Germans carry. "We have a feeling of responsibility, but we can't feel responsible,"[5] explains Lenz, a high school student.

After the war the Allies took control of different portions of Germany. Eventually Great Britain, France, and the United States united their sectors, forming a new democratic nation in West Germany, called the Federal Republic of Germany. To help the Federal Republic of Germany rebuild, the United States provided it with money. East Germany was controlled by the Soviet Union. It was set up as a Communist nation known as the German Democratic Republic. The city of Berlin was also split. In the ensuing years, West Germany flourished while East Germany stagnated.

Between 1948 and 1961 almost 3 million refugees from East Germany flooded into West Germany in search of a better life. Most crossed the border in Berlin, which was the easiest place to enter West Germany. To stop the exodus, in 1961 the Soviet Union built a concrete wall, guarded by armed soldiers, dividing East and West Berlin. Other border crossings between the two Germanys were fenced off and implanted with land mines to deter crossings. East Germans became virtual prisoners. They remained trapped until November 9, 1989, when changes in Soviet politics made travel out of East Germany legal. Hearing the good news, tens of thousands of East and West Germans flocked to the wall and, amid wild partying, began tearing it down. In 1990 the two Germanys were finally reunited into one nation. Since reunification, Germany has become an economic superpower and a voice for global peace and tolerance.

Government

Reunified Germany is a democracy whose official name is the Federal Republic of Germany. The nation is divided into sixteen *bundeslanders,* or states. Each state has its own governing entities, but the ultimate authority is the federal government, which is divided into three branches: legislative, executive, and judicial. The legislative branch consists of two houses: the Bundesrat and the Bundestag. Bundesrat members are appointed by the states, and Bundestag members are elected by German citizens, who are legally able to vote at the age of eighteen. Bundestag members elect the president and the chancellor. The chancellor is the head

Gestures and Body Language

Just as children learn oral language, they also learn distinctive gestures and body language that are specific to their culture. For instance, Germans show less emotion in their facial expressions than Americans, and they use gestures that may be unfamiliar to people of other cultures. For example, rather than crossing their fingers for good luck, Germans press their thumbs inside their fists and lightly pound on a hard surface to wish for good luck. Knocking is used to show appreciation. In response to presentations in academic, club, social, or work settings, Germans rap their knuckles on a hard surface like a table to show their approval; in these settings, applause may be perceived as mocking the presenter. For that reason, applause is restricted to theatrical performances.

Other gestures, which are often used in the United States, are avoided by Germans. For instance, putting the thumb and index fingers together to form the "okay" sign is considered a rude gesture.

of state, and the president's role is largely ceremonial. Members of both legislative houses select judges to serve on the Federal Constitutional Court, which is similar to the US Supreme Court.

As in all nations, governmental decisions affect the lives of all citizens, young and old. For instance, through a network of agencies, the government provides the German people with a generous social welfare system that includes universal health care, free college tuition, free vocational training, maternity benefits, and generous unemployment insurance. The system reduces the cost of living for individuals, allowing most Germans to maintain a comfortable lifestyle. As Christina, a high school teacher, explains, "I think it's good. . . . A parent takes responsibility for his or her children. A state [nation] takes responsibility for its citizens."[6]

Germans are also governed by policies established by the EU. The EU is an organization composed of twenty-eight European nations. It enacts policies designed to foster cooperation and economic prosperity among member nations. These policies address economic, environmental, security, human rights, and immigration issues, among others.

Membership in the EU provides German industries with trading partners eager for German products, which helps the local economy thrive. EU members also share a common currency—the euro—and are free to travel, live, work, and study in all member nations without any special visas or passports. Many German teens take advantage of these benefits.

An Aging Population

As of 2016, the population of Germany was 80,722,792, making it the most populous nation in Europe. Approximately 77 percent of the population is over the age of twenty-five, putting young people in the minority. Moreover, because Germany's birth rate is declining and elderly Germans are dying, the population is shrinking. Indeed, there are currently not enough people to fill available jobs.

Although in the past most Germans shared the same ethnic background, contemporary Germany has an ethnically diverse population. Former president Joachim Gauck explains: "A look at our country shows how bizarre it is that some people cling to the idea that there could be such a thing as a homogenous, closed single-colored Germany. It's not easy to grasp what it is to be German—and it keeps changing."[7]

This diversity is due in part to the fact that Germany is the second-most popular destination for immigrants in the world. About 15 million residents are of non-German descent. The German government welcomes new arrivals to boost the workforce, and it helps them acculturate by providing them with free German language classes and other social services. Dilek Kolat, a government official, explains: "We don't look at migrants as a possible threat or a possible problem, but we look at them as potential. What can they bring to society?"[8]

Although a large part of Germany's foreign population consists of individuals from other EU nations, it includes people from non-EU nations too. Turks, who make up 2.4 percent of the population, are Germany's largest ethnic group not of German descent. Guest workers from Turkey immigrated to Germany in the

> "A look at our country shows how bizarre it is that some people cling to the idea that there could be such a thing as a homogenous, closed single-colored Germany. It's not easy to grasp what it is to be German—and it keeps changing."[7]
>
> —Former German president Joachim Gauck

1960s, and many have become German citizens. Other ethnic groups include Serbs, Albanians, Russians, and people from the Middle East. Among the latter are asylum seekers from war-torn countries. According to an article on the website of the German media outlet Deutsche Welle, "As a matter of principle, Germany grants asylum to people who are politically, religiously or ethnically persecuted."[9] In fact, between 2015 and 2016 Germany took in more than 1 million asylum seekers, most of whom were young people.

Cities and Towns

Approximately 75 percent of Germans live in urban areas. Germany has four cities with a population of 1 million or more. With 3.6 million people, Berlin, the nation's capital, is the most populous. Although numerous German structures were destroyed during World War II, many fine old buildings survived. After the war, some damaged buildings were restored, others were meticulously rebuilt from the rubble, and still others were replaced with modern architecture. As a result, contemporary German cities are a mix of ornate old buildings adorned with spires and sculpted gargoyles as well as sleek, ultramodern steel-and-glass masterpieces.

German cities are bustling places filled with flourishing businesses, baroque cathedrals, charming sidewalk cafés, restaurants serving international fare, and a thriving cultural scene. Young urban dwellers can take advantage of the many museums, theaters, concert halls, and nightclubs. There are also lots of small specialty shops and large chain stores for young shoppers to patronize. Most urban dwellers live in neighborhoods that are just a short walk, subway ride, or bus ride from the city center but are well removed from industrial areas.

German cities are very clean. There are trash cans and recycling bins on almost every corner, and environmentally conscious Germans make a point of using them. Graffiti is prohibited. However, young artists are free to decorate the remnants of the Berlin Wall that are still standing. In fact, what is left of the wall has become an open-air gallery that features the work of both international and local graffiti artists. Viewing the artwork is a popular activity.

German cities are not only clean but also safe. Streets are well lit, and it is usually safe for young people to walk around day or night. When walking is not possible, buses, subways, trams, and train lines make getting around easy. It is common to see unescorted children and adolescents on public transportation. Children and teens are also a familiar sight in the many city parks and green spaces equipped with playgrounds, soccer fields, bicycle paths, and hiking trails.

German towns and villages also have lots of green spaces. Most are surrounded by thick forests, mountains, rivers, and/or farms. Many were spared the devastation of World War II and look much as they did centuries ago. Quaint cobblestone lanes, romantic castles, and medieval buildings make visitors feel as if they have been transported back in time or onto the pages of a fairy tale. Erin, a Canadian writer living in Germany, describes the town of Rothenberg:

> When you think of cute medieval German towns, this is the one you probably have in your mind. It was the inspiration for Pinocchio's home village in the 1940 Disney film, and parts of *Harry Potter and the Deathly Hallows Parts 1 and 2* were filmed here. Founded in 1170, it has . . . half-timbered buildings, cobbled streets, and my favorite thing: the city wall. You can walk along the upper walkway of the city walls, peering out arrow slits, and imagining you're a city guard on watch. The wall also affords a wonderful bird's eye view of all the little gardens and courtyards among the red roofs of the town.[10]

Although German towns may look as if they are lost in time, they are equipped with electricity, modern water supply systems, cell phone reception, Internet access, satellite and cable television, and other up-to-date amenities. Moreover, the Autobahn, a superhighway that connects most German cities and towns, makes it easy for rural residents to travel to nearby cities quickly. So although life may be a little slower paced for youngsters growing up in German towns and villages, their lives are not that different from their urban peers.

Looking Toward the Future

Like all nations, Germany faces many challenges as it moves forward. One issue that concerns many young Germans is protecting the environment. Germany has a global reputation as a leader in environmental matters. Issues concerning climate change, biodiversity, pollution, recycling, and renewable energy are important to most Germans, particularly teens. In fact, the Green Party, a German environmentalist political party, counts many young Germans among its supporters. Likewise, more than seventy-five thousand young people are members of the international Youth Association for the Protection of Nature, making it the largest organization for young people in Germany. Members attend conferences and workshops and carry out environmental projects that span the globe. In fact, Germany's commitment to improving the environment at home and abroad is so strong that as of 2016, 32 percent of the energy generated in Germany came from renewable sources like wind and solar power. The nation plans to produce all of its electric power from renewable sources by 2050. In addition, Germany has committed to contributing the equivalent of approximately $3 billion to develop renewable energy in Africa. This interest in protecting the earth is not surprising. Many young Germans see themselves as both German and global citizens. They understand that their nation's actions have a far-reaching effect, and they are taking on the challenge of ensuring the effect is a positive one.

CHAPTER TWO

Cozy Home and Loving Family

Home and family are important to Germans and play a key role in German culture. Family members treat each other with love and respect. They share household responsibilities, and they have fun together. Children and teens are taught specific values that are an essential part of German culture. Once these values are learned, young people are given a lot of freedom.

Small Families

The population of Germany is shrinking. The birth rate is declining, and older Germans are dying. People are waiting longer to marry and become parents, and they are having fewer children than in the past. Consequently, most young people grow up in small families with older parents. The average marriage age is thirty-three for men and thirty-one for women. And mothers are, on average, twenty-nine when their first child is born, which puts Germany seventh in countries with the highest mean age of mothers at first birth.

Although 21 percent of German households are headed by a single woman, most youngsters grow up in traditional nuclear families made up of a mother, father, and one or two children. Indeed, one out of five families has only one child. Many young people live a short distance from their grandparents, aunts, uncles, and first cousins, making it easy for extended family members to visit each other often. However, since Germany is not that large in area and the Autobahn and train system connect most of the nation, it is not difficult for family members that do not live in the same region to get together for occasional visits, family gatherings, and special events.

Sixty-five percent of German mothers work outside the home. The government guarantees new parents fourteen months of paid leave, which can be shared between both parents or used by just one. This allows parents time to bond with their new baby before returning to work. Once this time is up, inexpensive day care facilities help working parents care for their children. Grandparents also pitch in whenever possible.

At home, family roles are usually not gender specific. Mothers and fathers share responsibilities. It is not unusual for fathers to cook, change diapers, or perform other activities that are considered women's work in many other cultures. And both partners usually share in decision making. Parenting is also shared. Children are taught specific values that are ingrained in German culture. These include dependability, honesty, orderliness, cleanliness, courtesy, and obedience. Classic German children's stories reinforce these lessons—often in a frightening

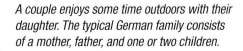

A couple enjoys some time outdoors with their daughter. The typical German family consists of a mother, father, and one or two children.

manner. For instance, in one story in the nineteenth-century children's book *Struwwelpeter*, a mother tells her son to stop sucking his thumb. When he refuses to stop, a tailor cuts off the child's thumbs, leaving him with bloody stumps. In another story, a mother tells her son to eat his soup. When the boy refuses to do so, he starves to death. The goal of such stories is to stop objectionable behavior. And the stories appear to work. According to Liv Hambrett, an Australian blogger living in Germany, "If you want to know why Germans are such direct, frank people with a deep appreciation for rules and the consequences of breaking them, look no further than their bedtime stories . . . the ones that promise punishment will be swiftly served, unless you do as your mother says."[11]

Although many modern German parents no longer read such disturbing tales to their children, the values the stories impart still play an important role in German life. Indeed, once learned, they

Family Pets

Most Germans are animal lovers. Pets, especially dogs, are treated like family members, and most young people grow up with a family dog. Dachshunds and German shepherds, two dog breeds that originated in Germany, are particularly popular. Germans spend a lot of time training their dogs, and most are well behaved. In fact, to ensure that dogs are not neglected, there are regulations concerning how much time dog owners must give their pet each day. Likewise, having dogs spayed or neutered and microchipped is required by law.

Dogs are allowed almost everywhere. Families often take their dogs to restaurants, where the pets sit quietly under the table. Often waiters place a dog dish full of water beside the animals. German dogs are also allowed in stores and on public transportation. The pets are typically so well trained that many walk unleashed on busy city streets. Although they may walk a few feet ahead of their masters, the dogs almost always keep their masters in view. And when they reach a crosswalk, they stop and sit until their owners say it is okay to cross the street. Dogs also accompany joggers as they trot through German parks. In fact, dogs are so beloved by Germans that it is not unusual for individuals to throw their pet a birthday party. Friends and family and their dogs are invited, and dog biscuits are served.

become second nature to most Germans. Says retired general Klaus Fruhhaber about one important German value, orderliness, "We are the perfect organizers. No muddling through. It is an inbred characteristic of the Germans to be organized. We learn it with our mother's milk."[12]

Once children have adopted these values, they are given a lot of freedom. Generally, German parents do not hover over their children. They trust them to make good decisions. As blogger Erin explains,

> "There are people who do not know their limitations, but most people have a beer or two casually. They don't get drunk."[14]
>
> —Spencer Cantrell, an American exchange student living in Germany

> I see kids my son's age (7) and a year or so younger, walking or taking the tram home from school on their own. . . . In the playgrounds, parents are sitting on benches, or picnic blankets hundreds of yards away while their kids play—and it's fine. . . . Interestingly, I very rarely see kids pushing ahead in the queue [line] for the slide, or not letting other kids have a turn on the swing—but they manage it themselves.[13]

Teens, in particular, are treated more like adults than like children. Parents trust teens to act responsibly and, for the most part, they do. For instance, the legal drinking age for beer and wine is sixteen, and the legal driving age is eighteen. But problems with teen alcoholism, binge drinking, or with young people drinking and driving are infrequent. As Spencer Cantrell, an American teen living in Germany, comments,

> A major difference in American and German culture is the drinking age. You must be 16 to drink wine and beer and 18 for liquor. Teens do drink in social situations. Of course, there are people who do not know their limitations, but most people have a beer or two casually. They don't get drunk. German teens are allowed to drive when they turn 18. . . . Teens seem to be careful about drinking and driving, too. When people go to the disco, their parents come to pick them up—at 1 a.m.—often in a carpool or something.[14]

Homes

Young Germans grow up in a variety of homes. Yet no matter the type, their homes provide them with a sense of *gemütlich* — comfort, coziness, and security. Space is at a premium in Germany, so most homes are small, and they are built quite close together. According to Ruth, an American blogger who lived in Germany for twelve years,

> For my west-coast American standards, it was very difficult to come to terms with what you can get for your money here. This is Germany: it is crowded, there are 80 million people in a country not quite as big as Oregon and Washington put together (which together have about 8 million people). The entire country is a bit like one big park, and all those people have to live somewhere. Entire neighborhoods and housing complexes are designed with the sole purpose of packing as many families onto as few square meters as possible.[15]

Even though most dwellings are small, they usually have several rooms, including an entryway; kitchen; dining room; living room; one to three bedrooms; a water closet, which is a room with a toilet and sink; and a separate room with a bath and/or shower. The compactness of these rooms helps create the sense of coziness that Germans love, as does the décor, which is likely to include overstuffed armchairs and sofas, cheery rugs and wallpaper, a cuckoo clock, and lots of knickknacks, houseplants, and family photos.

Homes in villages and small towns are typically freestanding and are often more spacious than those in larger cities. Big-city dwellers usually live in apartments or row houses. Typically, the latter are two-story houses with an attic and basement. As the name implies, the houses are attached to each other in one long row. About 64 percent of Germans own their homes or apartments. But even families

"Entire neighborhoods and housing complexes are designed with the sole purpose of packing as many families onto as few square meters as possible."[15]

—Ruth, an American blogger who lived in Germany for twelve years that rent their residences rarely move. One reason for this is that most rental properties do not include basic items such as closets, light fixtures, drapes, or carpeting. Kitchens are bare rooms, and bathrooms lack cabinetry. Renters must buy *kleiderschranks*—freestanding furniture that is used as closets—window coverings, and rugs. They also must buy and install cabinets, counters, shelves, light fixtures, and major appliances. Since this is costly, most renters tend to stay in one place. If they do move, they usually sell the equipment to the new tenant or take whatever items they can with them.

Although homes may come with only the bare essentials, almost all German homes have running water, electricity, and heat. Most have Internet access and cable or satellite television. Rooms are often individually heated. To save energy, Germans often heat only the rooms that they use, keeping the doors to unheated rooms closed. Keeping doors closed also enhances privacy in small residences, so doors to most rooms are kept shut even when heat loss is not a concern. This allows family members to retreat into a private space whenever they feel a need for solitude.

Teens typically have their own bedroom or share a room with a sibling. Decorations and furnishings are similar to what can be found in the bedrooms of American teens and are likely to include a bed, desk, *kleiderschrank*, books, posters, a computer, mp3 player, and other amenities that are part of modern teen life.

Privacy is important to Germans not only inside their homes but also outside them. Most houses have hedges or fences that separate them from their neighbors and provide a sense of privacy. Some homes have small gardens, a feature that many Germans covet. For those who do not have their own garden, most communities have areas set aside where people can lease garden plots. These plots may be only a few feet in area, but they are large enough for a flower or vegetable bed as well as a small toolshed. Tenants erect these sheds, which range from bare-bones huts to elaborate miniature houses. The sheds and the plots serve as family gathering spots where adults and children visit and work together. According to author Susan Stern, "On summer evenings and weekends, these areas are a flurry of gardening activity."[16]

Food

Another place where families gather is around the dining room table. No matter whether young Germans live in houses or apartments, it is likely that delicious aromas are coming from the kitchen. Germans love hearty food, and mealtime is when families connect. Mothers usually do the cooking, but it is not uncommon for fathers to pitch in.

Germans usually eat three meals and a few snacks a day. Breakfast begins with a hot beverage, such as cocoa, tea, or coffee. Typical breakfasts include muesli—a cereal made of grains, dried fruit, and nuts mixed with yogurt or milk—or ham or sausage served with a boiled egg and a fresh whole-grain roll spread with cheese. Indeed, Germans love bread. Bread and rolls are a part of almost every meal, and most Germans buy freshly baked whole-grain bread at least once a day. They have lots of varieties from which to choose. German bakers make more than two hundred different kinds of bread, all of which are baked fresh without any artificial preservatives. As author Peter Wortsman says, "Nobody knows how to bake whole grain bread like the Germans, it tastes like it just came out of the oven in Hansel and Gretel."[17]

> "Nobody knows how to bake whole grain bread like the Germans, it tastes like it just came out of the oven in Hansel and Gretel."[17]
>
> —Peter Wortsman, author

Breakfast is usually a shared meal. Many German families rise early so that they can eat breakfast together before rushing off to a busy day. Teens and children usually have a midmorning snack at school that they bring from home, typically a buttered roll and a piece of fruit or yogurt.

The school day usually ends in time for lunch. Traditionally, lunch is the main meal of the day and is eaten between noon and two in the afternoon. However, because of work schedules, many families have a hot meal for supper instead. But on the weekend, and whenever possible, families eat a large lunch together. A typical meal might consist of meat, particularly pork or chicken; potatoes; a vegetable, such as green beans or cabbage; hot bread; and a sweet dessert.

Supper, or *arbenbrot*, which means "light bread," is eaten around six or seven o'clock. It might consist of bread, cheese,

Three generations—grandparents, parents, and children—share a meal together in Berlin. Germans enjoy hearty food and savor mealtimes as a time to connect with family members.

sausage, sauerkraut, and pickles. Germans love sausage and make seventeen hundred different varieties. A fat, juicy sausage topped with mustard and accompanied by a hot roll or a big, soft pretzel also serves as a popular snack.

Other snacks are sweeter. To tide hungry Germans over between lunch and supper, many families have a late afternoon snack known as a *kaffeeklatsch*, with working families taking part in this afternoon ritual on the weekend. This is a time for children, teens, and adults to relax, spend time together, and share a beverage and a pastry. German pastries are world famous. Young people can indulge in treats such as a rich, chocolatey slice of Black Forest cake or a slice of coffee cake topped with fresh fruit, among other pastries.

Teens that are out and about after school or at night often frequent fast-food chains. These include many popular American fast-food chains that are found in most cities. Another very popular fast food is a *döner kebab*. This Turkish sandwich is made of slices of hot, juicy lamb or chicken that has been cooked on

Raising a Family

Germans raise their children to be responsible and independent. They do this without spanking, slapping, or other forms of corporal punishment, all of which are illegal in Germany. In fact, the government insists that children have a legal right to a violence-free upbringing. Similarly, corporal punishment is forbidden in day care facilities, schools, and juvenile correction centers. The law also prohibits adults from psychologically humiliating children.

The law was passed in 2000, making Germany the eleventh nation in Europe to enact this type of legislation. In total, thirty-five countries throughout the world have banned corporal punishment, and more than one hundred nations prohibit such actions in schools.

The German law is aimed less at punishing adult offenders than at helping them become better parents. Rather than facing imprisonment, parents and other adults who break the law usually are required to attend parenting classes to help them learn better child-rearing methods and therapy sessions that help them learn to manage anger.

a vertical spit, topped with salad and spicy yogurt sauce, and stuffed into a large piece of fluffy flatbread. Stands selling the delicious sandwich can be found all over Germany. Sometimes working parents buy the sandwiches as takeout and serve them for supper.

Good Neighbors

Germans have a strong sense of community. Families obey certain written and unwritten rules established by local communities concerning their home life. Most of these regulations are aimed at contributing to the public good, being considerate of one's neighbors, and maintaining an orderly environment. The rules affect what young people can and cannot do at home and in the neighborhood in which they live. For instance, most communities observe a quiet time so that residents who want to rest can do so without being disturbed. Quiet time occurs every day between one o'clock and three o'clock in the afternoon, after ten in the evening, and most of the day on Sunday. During quiet time, everyone is expected to keep the noise level to a minimum. As Stern explains, "Children are not supposed to play in the garden or in the street (not even quietly); household appliances of the loud vacuum-cleaner sort should not be used. Music must be played low. All must be absolutely quiet. . . . This is also true of evenings and Sundays. . . . Sunday is a day of such peace that the whole country practically closes down."[18]

Other regulations concern cleanliness and order. It is common for apartment dwellers to set up a rotating schedule for residents to clean interior and exterior common areas and shovel snow around the building. To make things more orderly, they typically allot each resident a specific day and time to use shared washing machines and clothes dryers located in the basements of apartment buildings. According to the website Passport to Trade 2.0, an online business etiquette guide, "Germans are most comfortable when they can organize and compartmentalize their world into controllable units. Time, therefore, is managed carefully, and calendars, schedules and agendas must be respected."[19]

The handling of trash, especially recyclables, involves rules too. Colored glass bottles are separated from clear ones and are placed in specifically designated trash containers. Plastic, paper, and metal also have their own individual trash bins. Moreover, in observance of noise rules, trash may be deposited only during nonquiet times. Although all these rules limit people's personal freedom, both young and old Germans are happy to follow them. "They see it contributing to the public good, their own included,"[20] explains author Barry Tomalin.

Having Fun Together

German family life is not all rules and regulations. German families like to have fun together. Sundays, in particular, are a time for families to do things together. In warm weather they flock to parks and wooded areas, where they picnic, walk, and bicycle. Indeed, taking a Sunday walk after a big lunch is a national pastime.

Going sailing is another warm-weather pleasure families enjoy. Many families that live near Germany's lakes own small sailboats. It is not unusual for family members to go out for a sail on the weekend or in the evening before eating supper.

In winter in Berlin (pictured) and elsewhere around the country, ice skating is a favorite family activity. In summer, many families enjoy sailing, bicycling, and picnics.

On Sundays in the winter, families often go ice skating or sledding together. On weeknights, families like to gather around the television and watch their favorite programs. Germans particularly enjoy reality television, talk shows, crime dramas, and American programs that are dubbed in German.

Taking family vacations is another way German families have fun together. Germans like to travel, and most workers have at least thirty days of vacation time a year. Taking a trip to the beach or going camping are popular ways to spend some of that time; so is visiting Germany's many zoos, national parks, and museums. But no matter what they do together, German families love, trust, and respect each other.

CHAPTER THREE

Education and Work for All

Throughout history, German schools have produced some of the world's most influential composers, philosophers, scientists, and artists. Germans value education. With an estimated literacy rate of 99 percent for individuals age fifteen and older, Germany spends more money on education than any other nation in Europe. No matter what young Germans aspire to be, the nation's educational system helps to prepare them for the future.

Getting an Education

Education is compulsory for youth ages six through eighteen, but many young Germans start school earlier. Children ages three through five can attend public kindergartens. In fact, the concept of kindergarten was invented in Germany as a way to help children adjust to being away from home before formally starting elementary school.

All children start elementary school at age six, and a child's first day of elementary school is an important rite of passage. To mark the occasion, entering first-graders are treated like celebrities. Each child is given a large decorated paper cone filled with candy, pencils, and small toys, and his or her picture is taken. The photos become family treasures that are proudly displayed in many homes. Some families hold a party to celebrate the event.

Children attend elementary school for four to six years, depending on the state. Each state administers its own schools. Although Germany has both public and private schools, the majority of youngsters attend public schools. Public schools are usually well maintained and well equipped. Class sizes are kept low, allowing teachers to give students individual attention. According to author Nicole Pfaff, "Classes are normally between 15 to 30 students, depending on the type of school. Class sizes are fixed and usually don't vary between grades and classes. Every class has its own room."[21]

While there are variations in school systems from state to state, the atmosphere, length of the school day, and curriculum does not differ significantly. Starting in first grade, all students study English as a foreign language. Other subjects are language arts, math, science, social studies, art, music, physical and health education, and computer skills. Yet despite the subject matter, the emphasis, especially in elementary school, is on enjoying learning in a comfortable, low-stress environment. As German educator Anja Abney explains, "In Germany there is an awareness of letting children be children while they learn," said Abney. "Teaching the whole person is much more what we do in Germany."[22]

On the first day of school first graders pose for photos with their decorated paper cones that are filled with candy, pencils, and toys. Photos taken by parents on this occasion become treasured mementos of childhood.

German students attend school five days a week, typically only in the morning. Although school hours depend on the state, in most areas students are dismissed for the day in time for lunch. "School starts here at 7:40," says Petra, who lives in southern Germany. "It finishes at 11:50. Yes, you read correctly, 11:50. A.M."[23] In addition, students get ample vacations. Schools in most states close for six weeks in the summer, one week in the fall, two weeks during the Christmas season, two weeks for Easter, and two weeks in June.

> "In Germany there is an awareness of letting children be children while they learn. Teaching the whole person is much more what we do in Germany."[22]
>
> —Anja Abney, a German educator

Students are not required to wear uniforms or follow any dress codes. And the atmosphere is fairly relaxed. As Spencer Cantrell explains, "Everyone wears jeans. . . . Guys often have jeans that would be considered tight by American standards. People wear Converse shoes and Dockers, often in outrageous colors. . . . Interesting scarfs are very popular among girls."[24]

Students are expected to behave responsibly, and most do. Rather than being confined in neatly aligned rows of desks, they sit at tables arranged in a semicircle, which helps foster group work and discussions, both of which are typical learning methods. Secondary school classes last forty-five minutes, and students attend four or five classes each day. Some classes meet three times a week, but others meet only once or twice a week. Students might study German, history, math, and chemistry on Monday, for example, and English, computer skills, and art the next day. Secondary students are given five-minute breaks between classes and fifteen-minute breaks after the second and fourth class. Students over the age of fourteen are free to leave the campus during these breaks. "Things don't seem as strict over here," Cantrell says. "You are allowed to have CD players, as long as you are respectful of the teacher and don't use them during class."[25]

Grades are given on a scale of one to six, with one being the equivalent of an A and six being the equivalent of an F. And although schools dismiss in time for lunch, students have homework every day. The amount varies by grade level. Most teens spend about one to two hours a night on homework. As Maike, a teenage girl from Klosterfelde, a town near Berlin, explains, "We really get a lot of homeworks, I don't like it because I sit at my desk to do them every day for more than 2 hours and when I've finished them, it's 7 o'clock. It's terrible."[26] Schools rarely have sports teams or after-school activities, but field trips are popular. Often, these are overnight outings to historical or cultural sites that relate to the students' studies.

Choosing a Path

When students complete elementary school, they move on to secondary school. This is a very important time—students, with the aid of their parents, must decide in which type of secondary school they want to continue their education. There are four types of secondary schools: *hauptschule,* gymnasium*, realschule*, and *gesamtschule;* each school prepares students for the future in different ways. Hauptschule is geared toward students with lower academic abilities. The emphasis is on hands-on learning and vocational training. Students are taught the same academic subjects as their peers in other types of schools but at a more basic level and at a slower pace. Additional subjects have a vocational orientation. About 25 percent of German students attend hauptschule. Students graduate when they complete ninth grade. Most then participate in an apprenticeship program, which combines on-the-job training with part-time enrollment in a vocational training institute.

About 24 percent of German students attend realschule, which is more academically rigorous than hauptschule. Students attend realschule through tenth grade. They take the same coursework as college-bound students, as well as applied sciences and vocational, business, and technical courses. Upon graduating, most students go on to attend a vocational or technical institute full-time. Others participate in an apprenticeship program. Some students transfer to a gymnasium, which prepares them for college.

Gesamtschules, or comprehensive schools, are a relatively new concept in Germany. These schools are not found in every state. Comprehensive schools enroll students of all ability levels, combining the coursework of hauptschule*,* realschule, and the gymnasium. Comprehensive school students graduate in grade nine, ten, or twelve, depending on their course of study. They then follow the same path as their hauptschule, realschule, or gymnasium peers, depending on their course of study and the duration of their school career.

The final type of school is the gymnasium, which prepares students for college. Approximately 30 percent of students attend a gymnasium. Students attend gymnasium through grade twelve or thirteen, depending on the state. Up until eleventh grade, students study liberal arts classes such as German, English, chemistry, philosophy, and history. According to Michelle, a Berlin teen, "We learn the basics like math, science, English, geography and a [foreign] language. Most students like to take an art course as well. We learn about the lives and cultures of people in other countries in history, geography and sometimes in science."[27] Upon entering eleventh grade, students choose a field of

Students take a test in French class at one of the country's college prep schools, known as gymnasiums. Those who score well on final exams and maintain good grades on their school work are guaranteed admission to the university of their choice.

specialization that their studies will focus upon for the remainder of secondary school. The most common fields of specialization are math-science, modern languages, and humanities.

Toward the end of their final year, gymnasium students are administered a written and oral exam known as the *abitur*, which tests their knowledge of their field of specialization. Students' test scores are combined with the grades they received in grades eleven and twelve (and grade thirteen in some cases) to obtain a composite score similar to a grade point average. This score is weighted, making it complicated to explain how the final number is determined. Passing composite scores fall between 280 and 820. Students obtaining a score in this range receive an abitur certificate, which guarantees admittance to the university of their choice.

Going On to College

All students with an abitur certificate can enroll in a public college or university. Germany has private colleges, too. But most students prefer to attend tuition-free public colleges. Tuition is also free for qualified foreign students. Young people pay only for their textbooks and their room and board. "College education in the U.S. is seen as privilege and expected to cost money and in Germany it is seen as an extension of a free high school education where one expects it to be provided," says Jeffrey Peck, the dean of the Weissman School of Arts and Sciences at New York's Baruch College. "It's a totally different attitude in what we expect as a society."[28]

"College education in the U.S. is seen as privilege and expected to cost money and in Germany it is seen as an extension of a free high school education where one expects it to be provided."[28]

—Jeffrey Peck, dean of the Weissman School of Arts and Sciences at New York's Baruch College

Before enrolling, students must declare a major. The number of open slots in each major varies, and competition for a place in a popular field like medicine can be intense. Therefore, although students are guaranteed admittance to college, to enroll in their preferred school they may have to select a less popular major or attend another college that has openings in their desired major.

From day one, the coursework focuses on a student's major field. College students are considered adults and are treated as such. They, according to authors Cath-

Military Service

Germany has its own army, air force, and navy, which in total consists of about 285,000 active duty troops and 7,750 reserve troops. Military service is not compulsory, and it is open to both men and women. To enlist, adults must be between the ages of eighteen and twenty-three. Volunteers typically serve from eight to twenty-three months. During this time, troops are paid a salary, get free room and board, receive a Christmas bonus, and get severance pay at the end of their service period. To ensure that military service is right for new enlistees, volunteers begin their service with a six-month trial period. During this trial period, if an individual does not like serving, that person can leave the military without any penalty.

Young Germans who have attended a vocational institute or have apprenticed in a particular trade or craft have the option of becoming noncommissioned officers. They usually serve for eight years, using their vocational training in a military setting.

Young men and women without specialized training who are willing to serve for eight to twelve years have the option of becoming sergeants. As sergeants, they perform managerial tasks and serve in a leadership role. Sergeants and other noncommissioned officers can rise through the ranks and become commissioned officers, many of whom make the military their career.

erine C. Fraser and Dierk O. Hoffmann, "have to learn to budget their own time and be aware of their academic progress—or lack thereof. Therefore, the emphasis is then placed on independent research (and not classwork) as well as on final comprehensive exams and extensive research papers."[29]

Most classes are held in large lecture halls. Attendance is not taken, and students are not penalized for missing classes. As journalist Rebecca Schuman explains,

> A freshman-level literature class in the United States might have 25 students registered, and a professor who is expected to know all of them by face and name by, say, week two. . . . A similar lower-level Vorlesung (lecture) in Germany might have an ever-changing coterie of 200 or so students, who show up when it suits them. (Yes, that includes milling into and out of the lecture hall at any point during the advertised class period.)[30]

Whenever possible, students live at home while attending college. When this is not an option, students often share an apartment near the university. A small minority live in college dorms. However, the number of dorm rooms is extremely limited, and the rooms themselves are quite basic. The campuses, too, offer few amenities. Schuman reports that "German universities consist almost entirely of classroom buildings and libraries—no palatial gyms with rock walls and water parks; no team sports facilities; no billion-dollar student unions with flat-screen TVs and first-run movie theaters. And forget the resort-style dormitories."[31]

Extracurricular activities are also limited. German colleges rarely have sports teams or big on-campus events. Groups of students usually get together off campus over a beer or a snack to socialize. Felix von Wendorff, a Californian studying at Goethe University in Frankfurt, explains:

Coming from California, the land where college parties are almost as ubiquitous as sunshine, traffic jams and surfing, I naturally assumed that this was true everywhere. . . . College parties in Germany are different: going to a bar with a group of friends, drinking a few beers and talking about stuff. Maybe you meet someone new. This form of partying is much more sensible for your health, wallet and brain.[32]

Learning on the Job

Not all German teens attend college. Teens who graduate from a hauptschule, realschule, or gesamtschule, as well as those who do not qualify for an abitur certificate, often go on to attend a vocational or technical institute in preparation for their chosen career. Many of them also complete an apprenticeship. Apprenticeship programs are dual programs that combine actual work experience with classroom instruction. Apprentices learn valuable career skills through on-the-job training under the supervision of an experienced craftsperson while also receiving formal classroom instruction in their chosen field. About two-thirds of an apprentice's time is spent on the job, and the

A culinary school in northern Germany trains students in the skills they will need to become chefs. Apprenticeship programs provide training for German youths for jobs ranging from auto mechanics to violin making to cooking and baking.

rest is in the classroom. Apprentices are paid for their work, and classroom instruction is free. Most receive about one-third the starting wage of a qualified craftsperson, or the equivalent of about $1,000 a month. Apprenticeships typically last two to three years. At the end of this time, apprentices take an exam that tests their professional skills. Upon successfully completing the exam, students are certified to work in their chosen profession.

Children's University

German children can experience what it is like to be a college student well before they are old enough to actually attend college. Starting at age seven, children can attend special lectures given by professors at local universities. According to an article by Carsten Janke for the Goethe-Institut,

> They . . . hear a professor talking about a particular topic: Why do volcanoes spew fire? Why are some people rich and others poor? Why do we love vampires? Or why is school stupid? Often these are questions that children themselves have asked. Professors then attempt to give answers to the seemingly simple questions, using their expert knowledge. At the same time they have to use straightforward language so that all the children will understand the answer.

> The goal of the lectures is to stimulate the children's enjoyment of learning and spark their interest in attending college in the future. "These days, the job of children's universities is to make universities more open. . . . The idea is that children from families in which nobody has ever gone to university before should be made curious about doing a degree," says Karoline Iber, a children's university organizer.

Carsten Janke, "Children's Universities Playing Students for a Day," Goethe-Institut, September 2016. www.goethe.de.

Approximately 1.5 million young people train in apprenticeship programs each year. Programs are offered in a wide range of fields, including baking, violin making, plumbing, and auto mechanics, just to name a few. The skills apprentices learn make them extremely employable not just in Germany, where the demand for them is great, but also throughout the European Union. As Robin Dittmar, an apprentice aircraft mechanic, explains, "I could work anyplace in the world. I like the system here. I know that I will be a good aircraft mechanic when I'm out of the apprenticeship, so that's very cool to know."[33]

Gainfully Employed

In a poll in which young Germans were asked what they wanted most in life, 97 percent of those surveyed said that they want to be employed in a profession that makes them happy. When young Germans complete their education or apprenticeship, finding suitable employment is usually not a problem. As of 2017, Germany had an unemployment rate of only 3.8 percent. Its unemployment rate for individuals twenty-five and younger is 6.5 percent, which is the lowest unemployment rate for this age group in the EU. Moreover, as Germany's population continues to age and its birth rate continues to shrink, future youthful unemployment in Germany is predicted to dip even lower. Currently, the demand for workers in many fields far exceeds the number of applicants. In fact, approximately one-third of all companies cannot fill job openings. This is especially true for positions requiring skilled craftspeople, engineering and technology professionals, energy specialists, health care specialists, and scientists. Indeed, it is not uncommon for qualified job applicants to receive multiple job offers, allowing them to pick and choose the position that suits them best.

> "I could work anyplace in the world. I like the system here. I know that I will be a good aircraft mechanic when I'm out of the apprenticeship, so that's very cool to know."[33]
>
> —Robin Dittmar, an apprentice airplane mechanic

Once graduates are hired, they usually find that they have a good work-life balance. Working overtime and taking work home is frowned upon. German workers are expected to arrive at work on time and work diligently throughout the day. When the workday is done, though, they are not expected to deal with work issues. In fact, in 2013 German civil servants received a directive that stated that workers should not work or open work e-mails on weekends, so that they have ample time to rest. Says author Barry Tomalin,

> Many people think that the Germans, like the Americans and increasingly the British, work every hour that God gives. In fact, they don't. For them overtime, staying late, and taking work home are signs of personal inefficiency. . . . For a German, the work ethic means that during your paid working hours you work as hard and in as disciplined and non-time-wasting a fashion as you can, but you don't

stay late. It also means reliability. You will be there when you say you will be, you will stop when you say you will, and you will do what you have said you will do. No more, but certainly no less.[34]

Additionally, young workers can expect to get at least twenty days of paid vacation annually. They also are entitled to up to six weeks of sick leave each year, and new parents get up to fourteen months of paid parental leave. Moreover, if German workers are laid off, which does not happen often, they receive generous unemployment compensation of a full month's salary for every year they were employed at the company. "Germany," says Raja, an Indian man working in Germany, "has a very good work culture. I love working here. . . . People encourage you if you have talent."[35]

Indeed, young Germans are educated to succeed. The nation's education system concentrates on and hones their talents. It prepares them for the world of work in a nation where unemployment is low and jobs are plentiful. And, once they are employed, their work life rarely conflicts with their leisure time.

CHAPTER FOUR

Social Life

German teens enjoy life. Most have lots of personal freedom and fill their leisure time with a variety of activities. Hanging out with friends, using social media, dating, participating in clubs, playing and watching sports, and traveling are just a few of the things they like to do.

Spending Time with Friends

Just like teens everywhere, German teens like spending time with friends. Most teens have a circle of friends that usually meet or communicate regularly. There is little separation between the sexes, so it is common for boys and girls to be friends and to be part of the same social group. Generally, teens have a lot of freedom. Most parents treat teenagers like adults, trusting them to make their own decisions, choose their own friends, and fill their leisure time in a responsible manner.

Many of the things teen friends do are similar to the type of things teens in many other Western countries enjoy. Activities such as hanging out in each other's homes, listening to music, going shopping, and going to a movie or out for ice cream are popular pastimes. Teens over the age of sixteen often visit local pubs, where they may have a cold beer, watch sporting events together, chat, and nibble on bar snacks. In warm weather, friends head outdoors to walk, hike, and bike in local parks. Many parks also have fitness circuits with chinning bars and balance beams, among other equipment, and some also provide Ping-Pong tables. Most communities have public swimming pools where young people gather in the summer. In the winter, friends often go ice skating and sledding. To warm up afterward, they head to a café for a hot beverage and a pastry. As a teenage girl explains,

Because my school is in the city I sometimes stay in the city and go shopping or just sit anywhere with my friends. When I'm at home I have to do stuff for school like homework but then I meet friends and we go to the ice cream shop or listen to music, talk, go to the swimming pool or hang out. In the evenings I like spending my time on my computer chatting to friends on facebook or icq [an instant messaging website] or such websites.[36]

When friends are not getting together, they communicate regularly via social media. According to *Deutschland Magazine*,

As in many countries, German teens enjoy hanging out with each other during their free time. And, as elsewhere, they rarely leave their mobile devices behind.

"Young people in Germany . . . use social networks extensively. Some 78% of 14- to 19-year-olds use online communities at least once a week and 76% of this age group visit forums, newsgroups or chatrooms every week. Social interaction with other Web users is the most important reason for young people to access the Internet."[37]

About 90 percent of Germans ages fourteen to twenty-nine are registered on at least one social media site. German teens are on Facebook, YouTube, Twitter, and Instagram, among other sites. In fact, Facebook has about 7 million registered German users. According to fifteen-year-old Michelle Buchholz, "Almost everybody has an iPhone or iPod. Facebook is very popular here too."[38]

SchülerVZ, a German social networking website with more than 5 million registered members, is also popular. Membership is limited to young people between the ages of twelve and twenty-one; members use the site to share photos, send messages, and chat and socialize with friends.

> "Almost everybody has an iPhone or iPod. Facebook is very popular here too."[38]
>
> —Michelle Buchholz, a German teenager

Dating

Dating is another way that young Germans enjoy themselves. Couples often first meet at school or through mutual friends. Many share the same circle of friends and gradually move from a platonic friendship to a romantic relationship. Indeed, first dates usually involve going out in a group.

Once couples move from a platonic relationship to a romantic one, single dates follow. There are no hard-and-fast rules about who initiates a date. And where couples go on dates varies. Going out for coffee, to dinner, or to a movie are typical; so is going to a pub or visiting a dance club or other music venue. In fact, any activity related to music or dancing is very popular—with techno and hip-hop music among teen favorites. According to Spencer Cantrell,

> A lot of American/English bands are very popular in Germany, as well as German bands. There's a German form of MTV, with subtitles in German. . . . I think the typical American teen would find the way Germans dance to

popular music very conservative. And who knows what a German teen would think of American dancing. Germans just don't have as much contact with one another when they dance. Dancing is done in groups, which I think is easier and just as fun.[39]

And generally, no matter who initiates the date, when the check comes each person pays his or her own share. In Germany men and women have equal rights; both usually have their own money, and most females are quite independent. As blogger and Berlin resident Rory McLean explains, "The bill arrives and the German Romeo starts to add up exactly who has eaten what. . . . Most other societies, it must be said, ensure that the male leaves the restaurant table significantly poorer. My German friends say that this is merely the by-product of feminism; the unspoken assumption that since men and women are equal, it is an affront to women to pay their way."[40]

> "Since men and women are equal, it is an affront to women to pay their way."[40]
>
> —Rory McLean, a blogger and resident of Berlin

Joining a Club

Many friends and dating couples get to know each other at one of the countless clubs in the country. In fact, being a member of a club is a major way that German teens fill their leisure time. Most schools do not have sports teams or other after-school activities. Clubs related to sports, hobbies, and other special interests fill the void. Handball, hiking, and bowling are popular sports clubs. There are also choirs and a cappella groups as well as model train, painting, astronomy, and dog-lover clubs, to name just a few. Some clubs, like green awareness clubs, focus on social issues, and others concentrate on politics or religion. But one thing is certain, there is a club for practically every interest. Indeed, an estimated 60 percent of all Germans belong to at least one club. According to authors Catherine C. Fraser and Dierk O. Hoffmann, "It is said that if three Germans with the same interest get together, they will organize a club. And, certainly, Germany probably holds the top spot in the Guinness records in regard to the number and variety of clubs."[41]

Happy Birthday

Germans celebrate their birthdays much like people do in the United States. But there are some differences. For instance, instead of adult and teen birthday celebrants being taken out and feted by friends and family, the celebrant is expected to make the invitations and pick up the tab. Workers celebrating their birthday are expected to bring pastries and other treats to work on their special day to share with their peers.

Parents often throw birthday parties for children. In fact, the idea of children's birthday parties originated in Germany. Parties take place at home or in a park. There is a set beginning and end time that is strictly followed. Most parties have a theme, such as soccer or music. And outdoor and indoor games, such as scavenger and treasure hunts, are part of the plan. There is a birthday cake with candles, and guests bring gifts. Not only that, children are not given homework and are not expected to do household chores on their birthday.

Other birthday customs relate to specific birthdays. For example, it is common for friends to pour flour on the top of the heads of teens celebrating their sixteenth birthday. Cracking eggs over the heads of teens turning eighteen is another German custom.

Clubs may be privately organized by a group of like-minded people or may be sponsored by the community or a church. Members may be mixed ages, all adult or all teen, co-ed or single gender. No matter their differences, all members share a common interest that binds them together. In fact, it is common for club members to form lifelong bonds and become as close as family. As author Frederick Kempe explains, "Though these clubs revolve around some specific activity the friendships formed there often follow members through a lifetime. They vacation together, raise children together, and generally settle life's problems together."[42]

Sports

Sports clubs are especially popular with German teens. Most Germans are avid sports fans who enjoy participating in and watching sporting events. There are approximately ninety-one thousand sports clubs in Germany, with about 2.7 million members. Many of these clubs sponsor teams that compete in almost every sport imaginable. Young people ski, ice skate, and play basketball, tennis, volleyball, and soccer, among other sports. They also like to get together in homes, pubs, and at stadiums to watch their favorite teams compete.

Soccer, or football as it is known in Europe, is far and away the most popular sport. As author Susan Stern points out, "No one single U.S. game can compete in popularity—you'd have to roll baseball, football, volleyball and ice hockey together to come close. . . . Young and old, from butcher and baker to egghead and surgeon, few are immune to the excitement of the matches."[43]

A televised soccer match captivates a group of boys in Berlin. The most popular sport in Germany, soccer draws many young people into youth leagues, and big matches routinely attract millions of spectators.

Germans are so passionate about soccer that it could be considered the national pastime. The German Football Association, which is the governing body for all amateur and professional soccer teams and leagues, is made up of more than 178,000 teams, including two professional soccer leagues that compete both nationally and internationally.

During the professional season, Germans are glued to their televisions watching the matches. And when Germany plays in the World Cup, even less-devoted sports fans get excited. In fact, during World Cup play in 2014, the atmosphere was electrifying. Teens and adults gathered for viewing parties in homes, pubs, and in front of big screens set up in outdoor areas. When the German team won, the nation erupted in celebration. World traveler Avanesh Gupta recalls,

> I was staying at Munich when Germany won the world cup. . . . Munich was decorated in Black, Red and Yellow [the colors of the German flag]. . . . Public views were arranged at a number of places, mostly Beergartens [beer gardens] and Pubs. Everyone was wearing at least one accessory to show their faith and support in Die Mannshaft [the men's national team]. People were flaunting their white German jersey and German flags. People were leaving their offices early and making up for their work later. . . . After the win, the roads were filled by people coming out of their houses, pubs, gatherings etc. shouting Deutschlaaaand [Germany] . . . Deutschlaaaaand!! There were people carrying the flags and the replica of [the] world cup. There were people sitting on the open windows of cars in all the major streets. . . . People were dancing, shouting and singing. . . . Music was played on the cars parked in the street and people were dancing throughout the boulevard.[44]

Not surprisingly, professional soccer players are huge celebrities and serve as role models for German youth, many of whom dream of following in their idols' footsteps. Many German boys and girls start playing soccer almost as soon as they can dribble a ball. Children as young as four can join a youth soccer club and be part of an age-appropriate team. Boys and girls play together on youth teams until age fifteen, when teams become gender specific.

Although many young people play soccer just for fun in parks and streets, youth club teams are taken seriously. Germany has a standardized national youth soccer curriculum that club coaches follow. Starting at age six, all club soccer members are taught specific skills based on their age. The goal, according to sports blogger Stuart James, is "identifying promising youngsters and providing them with technical skills and tactical knowledge at an early age."[45]

In fact, many of Germany's best soccer players started out as soccer club members. Athletes as young as eight are monitored by scouts from professional teams who can often be found on the sidelines of club matches. Once they are teenagers, the most talented youngsters are invited to participate in special training programs run by professional teams, which spend the equivalent of about $92 million annually on these programs. The goal is to produce future soccer stars.

To become good enough to participate in such programs, youngsters must train hard. Most youth teams practice twice a week for ninety minutes per session, year-round. Some teams practice indoors in the winter, but many brave rain, snow, and ice to practice outdoors. Games are played every Saturday from September through June, with a typical season consisting of about thirty games. Moreover, each soccer club has its own soccer fields with locker rooms, showers, a meeting room, and often a snack bar or restaurant. Most have websites where they post information about the teams, the club sponsors, and the team members. As German author and soccer expert Gunther Karsten explains,

> In Germany every club puts photos of all teams on their website and often also the names (although often only the capital of the last name for security reasons) and photos of all players. And the very good soccer clubs (who are very active in developing the young players) even write down the size, weight, the position, successes and motto of the kid. What a motivation for a kid to be presented in that way—almost like a professional player![46]

CHAPTER FIVE

Religious Influences

Christianity has been a part of German culture for centuries. In fact, the Protestant Reformation, a sixteenth-century religious movement that began as an attempt to reform the Catholic Church and resulted in the creation of Protestantism, took place in Germany. As a result, some of the nation-states that were united to form what is now Germany adopted Protestantism, but others remained Catholic. Today approximately 68 percent of all Germans identify as Christians. Of these individuals, about half identify as Catholic and half identify as Protestant. Twenty-eight percent of Germans, on the other hand, say they are not a follower of any religion. For many young Germans, religion is more about customs and traditions than strict adherence to religious teachings. According to German cleric Hanfried Zimmermann, even though a majority of Germans identify as Christians, it "doesn't mean that most people are faithful churchgoers, only that the tradition is still intact."[51]

Even many devout young people tend to pick and choose what religious rules they follow. Many teens believe that religious doctrine is fluid and should be interpreted to reflect contemporary values. Consequently, they reject religious teachings that they feel do not promote public health, tolerance, or social justice—contemporary values that most young Germans hold dear.

Premarital Sex

Christianity prohibits premarital sex. Nonetheless, many German teens are sexually active. As a society, Germans consider teen sexual activity a public health issue rather than a religious one. Most Germans view youthful sexual activity as a natural part of

Young people in southwest Germany take part in a confirmation ceremony at their church. Many Germans identify as Christians, but the country's young people (even those who are devout) tend to pick and choose which religious teachings to follow.

human development and are accepting of teens being sexually active as long as they act responsibly. In fact, it is not uncommon for German parents to allow a teen to have their boyfriend or girl-friend spend the night.

A report by the World Health Organization reveals that 33.5 percent of fifteen-year-old girls and 22.5 percent of fifteen-year-old boys in Germany are sexually active. Of these, approximately 95 percent of the girls and 88 percent of the boys reported that they used con-traceptives the last time they had sex. According to an article on the website Advocates for Youth, in Germany "young people believe it is 'stupid and irresponsible' to have sex without protection. Youth rely on the maxim, 'safer sex or no sex.' Society weighs the morality of sexual behavior through an individual ethic that includes the values of responsibility, respect, tolerance, and equity."[52]

Indeed, most young people are knowledgeable about human sexuality long before they enter into a physical relationship. Starting in first grade, German youth receive comprehensive sex education in school and through public education campaigns. These campaigns, according to Advocates for Youth, "are direct and humorous and focus on both safety and pleasure."[53]

In schools, sex education is a required part of the science and health curriculum. Parents cannot opt children out of the classes for any reason. The curriculum is based on the students' age and includes information about sexually transmitted diseases, pregnancy, contraception, homosexuality, and making responsible choices, among other topics. It also promotes tolerance of individuals with alternative sexual orientations.

In addition to receiving comprehensive sex education, German teens have easy access to contraceptives. All usual methods of contraception are available in Germany. Condoms and emergency contraception (the morning-after pill) are sold over the counter in almost every drugstore. Other birth control methods, such as birth control pills, intrauterine devices, and diaphragms, require a doctor's prescription. However, getting a prescription is simple, and the doctor's fee is covered by Germany's national health insurance.

> "Young people believe it is 'stupid and irresponsible' to have sex without protection. Youth rely on the maxim, 'safer sex or no sex.'"[52]
>
> —Advocates for Youth, an organization that promotes teen sexual health

Abortion

Most sexually active German teens practice safe sex. The annual birth rate for women age fifteen to nineteen is 8.2 per 1,000 births. (In comparison, the US rate for the same age group is 34.2.) Even though teen pregnancy rates are low, unwanted pregnancies still occur. To terminate an unwanted pregnancy, some women seek an abortion. Abortion rights are controversial in Germany. Christian doctrine says that life begins at conception; therefore, it prohibits the procedure. Some Germans accept this doctrine, but others consider abortion to be an issue of public health and women's rights. In an effort to find common ground between these two camps, Germany does not have a formal law that makes abortions legal. However, if women meet certain requirements, they can undergo the procedure without threat of punishment.

Germany's Growing Muslim Population

Germany has a growing Muslim population. As of 2016, 3.7 percent of the population identified as Muslim. This translates to nearly 6 million people. Most of these individuals are economic immigrants from the Balkans, including Albania and Kosovo, and asylum seekers from North Africa and the Middle East. In fact, approximately 1 million Muslim migrants arrived in Germany between 2015 and 2016. Many were teens and young adults.

Muslims are free to practice their religion in Germany, and Islam is currently the fastest-growing religion in the country. To accommodate this growth, a number of churches are being converted into mosques, some of which publicly sound calls to prayer from outdoor loudspeaker systems.

Most Germans welcome these new arrivals, but there is some backlash to their growing numbers. Some Germans worry that some of these migrants may be terrorists. Another problem is that some Islamic laws and traditions conflict with German culture. For instance, many migrants adhere to sharia law—civil law based on the teaching of the Koran—and sharia courts have been set up in some German cities. Some Germans feel this undermines German civil law. However, despite these misgivings, the government is working hard to help the country's Muslim population fully integrate into society.

As of 2017, the annual abortion rate in Germany among pregnant women age fifteen to nineteen was 6.1 per 1,000. Women must meet certain requirements before having an abortion. Once the requirements are met, the procedure is readily available for up to twelve weeks after conception for general pregnancies and for up to twenty-two weeks after conception for cases in which the mother's life is in danger. To meet the requirements, a health care professional must determine the stage of pregnancy and the woman must attend a counseling session at a licensed counseling center. Three days after the counseling session, she can get an abortion from a medical doctor in a hospital or other safe, clean health facility without any legal repercussions. The cost of the procedure is not covered under the national health insurance system.

Homosexuality and Gay Rights

Homosexuality and gay rights is another area in which religious doctrine conflicts with the values that many German teens respect. Although Christianity prohibits homosexual behavior, many young Germans believe that tolerance and acceptance of people with diverse lifestyles takes priority over religious law. Therefore, although there is resistance to homosexuals among some religiously conservative individuals, for the most part young gays and lesbians are accepted by society. In fact, in a 2013 Pew Research survey, 87 percent of Germans surveyed said that society should accept homosexuality. Out of thirty-nine countries participating in the survey, Germany ranked second in acceptance of homosexuality. Another survey, this one conducted by the German news magazine *Stern* in 2013, found that 74 percent of Germans support same-sex marriage.

Despite public support, same-sex marriage is not legal in Germany. However, registered partnerships or civil unions between same-sex couples are legal, and the law provides these couples with the same tax and social welfare benefits as traditionally married couples. And lesbians, gays, bisexuals, and transsexuals are guaranteed the same legal rights as heterosexuals. This means they cannot be discriminated against in housing, employment, or other aspects of daily life. In addition, hate crimes against homosexuals, ranging from verbal assaults to violence, are forbidden. As Bastian Finke, who runs the Berlin gay-rights group Maneo, says, "We have standards in Germany, we have laws against hate crimes here."[54]

> "We have standards in Germany, we have laws against hate crimes here."[54]
>
> —Bastian Finke of the Berlin gay-rights group Maneo

Indeed, sexually diverse lifestyles are accepted by most young Germans. In fact, many young people go out of their way to show their support. As an example, author Peter Wortsman describes one neighborhood in Berlin largely populated by young adults: "This once rundown east Berlin working class district turned bohemian hub had evolved into a gentrified nexus of cafes, hi-end boutiques, and refurbished pre-war facades, its balconies bedecked with plants and draped with rainbow Gay Pride banners and other insignia of tolerance."[55]

Most German cities have a large and open gay community that encompasses nightclubs, bars, hotels, saunas, restaurants, shops, and publications that are run by and cater to homosexuals. Berlin, in particular, is famous for its large homosexual

A gay rights march in Dresden in 2017 draws a large crowd. Although same-sex marriage is not legal in Germany, young gays and lesbians generally find acceptance in their country.

community. It is estimated that approximately five hundred thousand gays and lesbians live there. The city hosts many gay festivals, parties, and other special events. It is also the home of a national monument dedicated to the thousands of homosexuals who were persecuted by the Nazis.

Globally, Germany is considered to be a gay-friendly nation. In fact, it has become a haven for many young homosexuals fleeing nations in the Middle East and Africa where homosexuals face imprisonment. As a persecuted group, these individuals receive asylum in Germany and other EU nations.

Rites of Passage

Even though many German teens do not accept all religious doctrine, religious traditions play an important role in German culture. Many rites of passage, including baptisms, first communions, and confirmations, are tied to Christian teaching. Infants are introduced into the Christian faith through baptism. At eight years old, many children receive their first Holy Communion. During this ceremony, which takes place in church, children receive the sacrament of the Eucharist. This sacrament involves eating a blessed wafer and taking a sip of wine; the wafer and wine symbolize the body and blood of Jesus Christ. To prepare for it, children attend religious instruction classes sponsored by their church. These classes often include day-long retreats where youngsters learn about their religion through songs, games, and physical activities.

During their early to mid-teens, many young Catholics receive their confirmation. In this church ceremony, teens renew and affirm their religious faith with family and friends looking on. Teens wear new clothes for the occasion, and parents often take photos of the confirmand that they send out as postcards. The ceremony is typically followed by a family dinner or party during which the teen is feted with gifts.

In addition to its religious meaning, being confirmed marks a teen's transition from childhood to adulthood. In fact, many German teens that are not part of any organized religion go through a similar ceremony to mark their maturity. The ceremony, which is known as a *jugendweihe,* or youth consecration, is a secular ceremony modeled after a Christian confirmation. Brigitte Hillig, a mother who underwent the ceremony as a teen, explains that "it is a way of leading children towards their adult life, of showing them that they are coming to a turning point. They see that they are growing up and the ceremony is a way of marking this change."[56]

Jugendweihe, which is organized by a number of sectarian groups, including the German Humanist Association, is especially popular in the states that formerly made up East Germany, where one in every three teens participates in the event. All religious practices were banned in these states under Communist rule. Although freedom of religion is guaranteed under modern German law, the collapse of East Germany did not spark a religious revival in that part of the nation. The ceremony is also increasingly popular in the rest of the nation. In total, about fifty thousand teens participate in the event annually. According to journalist Tamsin Walker, "Supporters see it as a non-religious way to give teenagers a forum to expand their minds, horizons and understanding of morals."[57]

During the twenty-week period before the ceremony, teens attend classes and participate in workshops, field trips, and other activities that focus on morality, tolerance, ethics, and human rights. The ceremony itself is done in groups and is held in large outdoor venues. As in confirmations, participants wear new clothes, receive gifts, and are honored by their loved ones. Taking part in jugendweihe does not mean that teens become members of any humanist group. It is a once-in-a-lifetime experience that gives nonreligious teens a chance to celebrate their coming of age. Says Milan, a fifteen-year-old boy, of the experience, "To do this in a group with others and feel that I am a grown-up now was a good feeling."[58]

> "Supporters see [jugendweihe] as a non-religious way to give teenagers a forum to expand their minds, horizons and understanding of morals."[57]
>
> —Journalist Tamsin Walker

A Season of Traditions

Other important aspects of German culture are also tied to Christianity. Although many teens do not attend religious services or rigidly follow Christian teachings, Christian holidays, especially Christmas, are a part of their lives. The Christmas season is an especially festive time of year, filled with tradition, joy, fun, and family. Even young people who do not identify with any religion cherish the traditions and take part in the festivities. As James, a British blogger who lives in Germany, explains,

> "Christmas is a special time in Germany. . . . Whenever I am back in the U.K., I feel that Christmas has lost its magic. Just another opportunity for rampant consumerism to rear its ugly head and for spoilt kids to demand the latest toy or gadget. In Germany it's different. It's the whole ambience of the month of December and the feeling of celebrating a special time, where the old year comes to a close. Goose,

Glühwein [spiced wine] and good time spent with friends amongst the aromas of the Christmas market is a snug feeling in a foreign land. Even though religion plays absolutely no part in my life, I find myself in November looking forward to the start of [the] Christmas . . . season.[59]

The Christmas season begins with Advent, the four-week period before Christmas Day. To commemorate the season, Germans display a horizontal wreath, known as an Advent wreath, on a tabletop. Set on the wreath are four colored candles and one white candle in the center. The colored candles symbolize hope, peace, joy, and love, and the white candle represents the life of Jesus Christ or purity. On the first Sunday of Advent, families light a colored candle. An additional colored candle is lit on each Sunday, until all four candles are lit. Finally, all the candles, including

German Weddings

In Germany getting married often consists of two distinct ceremonies. First, there are the legal formalities. All couples must register six weeks before their wedding day in the local magistrate's office. The bride and groom both must be at least eighteen years old; younger couples must have written parental consent. Six weeks after registering, the couple returns to city hall, where they are married in a civil ceremony. Usually, only a small number of the couple's closest family attends. The ceremony makes the marriage official and is the only marriage ceremony required by law. Marriages performed by priests, ministers, imams, rabbis, or other religious leaders are not legally binding.

Days or even months later, many couples have a religious ceremony, too. Germans follow many traditions related to the religious ceremony. For instance, the night before the ceremony, the couple is expected to throw an informal party known as a *polterabend*. At this party the guests smash plates and dishes to bring the bride good luck. At the ceremony itself, the bride and groom exchange wedding rings, which are worn on the right hand. Afterward, the guests toss rice at the couple. It is said that the bride will have as many children as the number of grains of rice that stick to her hair. A reception with music, food, drink, dancing, and wedding cake usually follows the church ceremony.

the white candle, are lit on Christmas Eve. The idea for the wreath originated in Germany during the sixteenth century, and Germans have been following this tradition ever since.

Germans also display another German creation, an Advent calendar, in their homes during the holiday season. These special calendars, which were invented during the nineteenth century, are used to count down the days from the start of the Advent season to Christmas Day. The calendars resemble cardboard posters decorated with numbers for each day leading up to Christmas. Each number has a flap or window that is opened, usually by children, to reveal tiny gifts and seasonal images and poems. According to authors Catherine C. Fraser and Dierk O. Hoffmann, "Even those who have not been inside a church in years will mark each of the four Sundays of Advent by lighting an additional candle on a wreath displayed in the home and opening doors, envelopes, and pockets on an Advent calendar to find small gifts or see new images."[60]

Other Christmas traditions, such as Christmas trees and gingerbread houses, also originated in Germany and are still a part of Christmas celebrations there. One tradition, known as St. Nicholas Day, is especially significant. It is celebrated on the night of December 5. In anticipation of a visit from St. Nicholas, a fourth-century Christian saint with a reputation as a bringer of gifts, and his assistant Ruprecht, children leave out clean shoes. St. Nicholas fills the shoes with edible treats for children who have behaved well. Ruprecht fills them with a stack of twigs for those who have not.

On December 6, individuals dressed as St. Nicholas and Ruprecht visit kindergartens, primary schools, and youth clubs, where they distribute candy to young children. Many of these individuals are teens hired by families and institutions to play the part of the saint and his assistant. The teens are required to have costumes—a red-and-white suit and a long white beard for Saint Nicholas and a long brown hooded robe for Ruprecht. And they must attend a class that instructs them on how to deal with different situations that might arise. They are paid the equivalent of about $30 for each twenty-minute-long appearance and can earn up to the equivalent of $400 in a typical season. Teens frequently use this money to buy Christmas gifts for their loved ones. Germans usually exchange gifts on Christmas Eve.

Dressed in angel and St. Nicholas costumes, students from Berlin's universities take part in an annual gift drive and distribution around Christmas. Younger teens often don costumes and give out candy to children at this time of year.

One place where teens purchase gifts is at traditional Christmas markets. These are huge open-air markets held in almost every city and town square. Rows of wooden stalls, adorned with strings of twinkling lights, offer shoppers everything Germans associate with a traditional Christmas. There are seasonal foods like roasted chestnuts, gingerbread, Christmas cakes, and sugar-coated almonds, which Germans take home to share with their loved ones. Likewise, there are foods like sausage and hot apple cider for hungry shoppers to snack on. Musicians stroll through the markets playing Christmas carols. Artisans sell beautiful blown-glass Christmas ornaments, handmade wooden toys, and gold-foil angels, among other items. Katie, an American blogger married to a German, says, "There is spiced wine, happy children, and handmade Christmas crafts on display. I love the smell of roasting nuts and imagine the cinnamon and laughter. . . . It's the sort of celebration where you just want to go every day. You want to smell everything . . . and buy everything."[61]

Germans have been holding Christmas markets for more than seven hundred years. They are not only a shopping haven but also a social spot where both devout and nonreligious Germans share their culture. Indeed, even though many Germans do not adhere to all the teachings of Christianity, religion is a vital part of German culture and tradition. These traditions, along with the values of tolerance, responsibility, and social justice, strongly impact the lives of German teens.

SOURCE NOTES

Chapter One: A Progressive and Prosperous Nation

1. *Travel Blog,* "Germany." www.travelblog.org.
2. Quoted in *Expats Blog*, "American Expat Living in Germany—Interview with Eifel Mausi," November 23, 2016. www.expats blog.com.
3. Peter Wortsman, *Ghost Dance in Berlin*. Palo Alto, CA: Travelers Tales, 2013, p. 5.
4. Quoted in Frederick Kempe, *Father/Land*. New York: G.P. Putnam's Sons, 1999, p. 81.
5. Quoted in Kempe, *Father/Land,* p. 146.
6. Quoted in Kempe, *Father/Land,* p. 73.
7. Quoted in Jenny Hill, "Germany Struggles to Adapt to Immigrant Influx," BBC News, November 3, 2014. www.bbc.com.
8. Quoted in Hill, "Germany Struggles to Adapt to Immigrant Influx."
9. Matthias von Hein and Volker Wagener, "Germany from A to Z," Deutsche Welle, October 28, 2015. www.dw.com.
10. Erin McGann, "Visiting Rothenburg ob der Tauber with Kids," *Erin at Large* (blog), March 1, 2017. http://erinatlarge.com.

Chapter Two: Cozy Home and Loving Family

11. Liv Hambrett, "Cautionary Tales," *Liv Hambrett: An Australian Writer in (North*) Germany* (blog), June 6, 2012. www.livham brett.com.
12. Quoted in Kempe, *Father/Land,* p. 108.
13. Erin McGann, "Expat Kid: Adjusting to a New Life," *Erin at Large* (blog), March 5, 2017. http://erinatlarge.com.
14. Spencer Cantrell, "German Teens Are Different After All," Savannah Now, November 4, 2003. http://savannahnow.com.
15. Ruth, "Schaffe Schaffe Häusle Baue," *German Way & More* (blog), October 17, 2011. www.german-way.com.

16. Susan Stern, *The Strange German Ways*. Bonn, Germany: Atlantik-Brucke, 1994, p. 31.
17. Wortsman, *Ghost Dance in Berlin,* p. 2.
18. Stern, *The Strange German Ways,* pp. 23–24.
19. Quoted in Kim Ann Zimmermann, "German Culture: Facts, Customs, and Traditions," Live Science, January 23, 2015. www.livescience.com.
20. Barry Tomalin, *Germany*. London: Kuperard, 2008. p. 47.

Chapter Three: Education and Work for All

21. Nicole Pfaff, "Germany," in *Teen Life in Europe,* ed. Shirley Steinberg. Westport: CT: Greenwood, 2005, p. 92.
22. Quoted in Holly Young, "What We Can Learn from the Great German School Turnaround," *Guardian* (Manchester, UK), November 25, 2015. www.theguardian.com.
23. Quoted in *Jillian in Italy* (blog)*,* "A Kid's Life: Germany," December 11, 2012. https://jillianinitaly.com.
24. Cantrell, "German Teens Are Different After All."
25. Cantrell, "German Teens Are Different After All."
26. Maike Boysen, "Teenage Life in Germany," Silver International, 2005. http://silverinternational.mbhs.edu.
27. Quoted in Sara Anderson, "Teen Life in Germany vs. Teen Life in America," Prezi, June 1, 2011. https://prezi.com.
28. Quoted in Franz Strasser, "How US Students Get a University Degree for Free in Germany," BBC News, June 3, 2015. www.bbc.com.
29. Catherine C. Fraser and Dierk O. Hoffmann, *Pop Culture Germany!* Santa Barbara, CA: ABC-CLIO, 2006, p. 87.
30. Rebecca Schuman, "You Can Now Go to College in Germany for Free, No Matter Where You're From," *Browbeat* (blog), *Slate*, October 10, 2014. www.slate.com.
31. Schuman, "You Can Now Go to College in Germany for Free, No Matter Where You're From."
32. Felix von Wendorff, "Student Life in Germany," *Top Universities Student Blog*, February 13, 2014. www.topuniversities.com.

33. Quoted in Eric Westervelt, "The Secret to Germany's Low Youth Unemployment," NPR, April 4, 2012. www.npr.org.

34. Tomalin, *Germany*, pp. 48–49.

35. Quoted in Mithila Borker, "Germany Has a Very Good Work Culture," Local, April 22, 2013. www.thelocal.de.

Chapter Four: Social Life

36. *Teenage Life in Germany* (blog), "The Typical Day of Teenage Girl in Germany," June 7, 2010. https://islaviviengermany.wordpress.com.

37. Quoted in German Missions in the United States, "Youth and Social Networks." www.germany.info.

38. Quoted in Anderson, "Teen Life in Germany vs. Teen Life in America."

39. Cantrell, "German Teens Are Different After All."

40. Rory MacLean, "The New Frugality," Goethe-Institut, November 2008. www.goethe.de.

41. Fraser and Hoffmann, *Pop Culture Germany!,* p. 155.

42. Kempe, *Father/Land,* p. 41.

43. Stern, *The Strange German Ways,* p. 94.

44. Avanesh Gupta, "What Was It Like to Be in Germany When Germany Won the World Cup?," Quora, January 28, 2015. www.quora.com.

45. Stuart James, "How Germany Went from Bust to Boom on the Talent Production Line," *Guardian* (Manchester, UK), May 23, 2013. www.theguardian.com.

46. Quoted in John Napier, "Youth Soccer Comparison: USA vs. Germany," Goal Nation, January 4, 2015. http://goalnation.com.

47. Robin Alexander, "German Soccer Fans Need Some US Manners," *Chicago Tribune*, September 3, 2014. www.chicagotribune.com.

48. Live Work Germany, "15 Random Things About Germany Which I Love," March 19, 2017. http://liveworkgermany.com.

49. *Der Spiegel,* "Party to End for Mallorca's German Tourists," July 22, 2013. www.spiegel.de.

50. Quoted in Caitlan Reeg, "Volunteer Abroad with Kulturweit or Weltwärts," Young Germany, July 11, 2016. www.young-germany.de.

Chapter Five: Religious Influences

51. Quoted in Lucian Kim, "Why East German Teens Seek Secular Rite of Passage," *Christian Science Monitor,* May 12, 1999. www.csmonitor.com.
52. Advocates for Youth, "Adolescent Sexual Health in Europe and the US." www.advocatesforyouth.org.
53. Advocates for Youth, "Adolescent Sexual Health in Europe and the US."
54. Quoted in Michael Scott Moore, "Does Germany Have a Problem with Gay Hate Crime?," *Der Speigel,* July 3, 2008. www.spiegel.de.
55. Wortsman, *Ghost Dance in Berlin,* p. 109.
56. Quoted in Tamsin Walker, "A Secular Rite of Passage," Deutsche Welle, March 14, 2005. www.dw.com.
57. Walker, "A Secular Rite of Passage."
58. Quoted in Bhavya Dore, "In Germany Secular 'Confirmation' Thrives Again," *Deseret News* (Salt Lake City), July 22, 2016. www.deseretnews.com.
59. Live Work Germany, "15 Random Things About Germany Which I Love."
60. Fraser and Hoffmann, *Pop Culture Germany!,* pp. 161–62.
61. Making This Home, "Life Abroad: German Christmas Markets," December 22, 2008. www.makingthishome.com.

FOR FURTHER RESEARCH

Books

Alan Farmer and Andrina Stiles, *The Unification of Germany and the Challenge of Nationalism, 1789–1919.* London: Trans-Atlantic, 2015.

Hal Marcovitz, *Life in Nazi Germany.* San Diego: ReferencePoint, 2015.

John Perritano, *Germany.* Broomall, PA: Mason Crest, 2015.

Ida Walker and Shaina C. Indovino, *Germany*. Broomall, PA: Mason Crest, 2012.

Christine Zuchora-Walske, *The Berlin Wall*. Edina, MN: Abdo, 2014.

Internet Sources

Central Intelligence Agency, "Europe: Germany," *The World Factbook,* 2016. www.cia.gov/library/publications/the-world-factbook/geos/gm.html.

CountryReports, "Germany Facts and Culture." www.countryreports.org/country/Germany.htm.

Deutsche Welle, "Germany." www.dw.com/en/top-stories/germany/s-1432.

Fact Monster, "Germany." www.factmonster.com/country/germany.

HistoryWorld, "History of Germany." www.historyworld.net/wrldhis/PlainTextHistories.asp?historyid=ac62.

Websites

Deutschland.de (www.deutschland.de/en). Deutschland.de is run in cooperation with the Federal Foreign Office in Berlin. It offers information for foreigners on German politics, economics, daily life, culture, and environmental concerns as well as a blog.

European Union (http://europa.eu). This is the official website of the European Union. In addition to general information about the EU, there is a large section on Germany and its role in the organization.

German Culture (http://germanculture.com.ua). This website provides all sorts of information about German culture, including information on traditions, food, and history.

German Missions in the United States (www.germany.info). This is the official website of German Missions in the United States (consulates, embassies, etc.). It offers news articles about Germany and lots of information about German life and culture. It also includes information about studying in Germany.

Goethe-Institut (www.goethe.de/en). The Goethe-Institut is a German cultural institute. Its website provides lots of articles about German life and culture.

INDEX

PICTURE CREDITS

ABOUT THE AUTHOR

Barbara Sheen is the author of ninety-seven nonfiction books for young people. She lives in New Mexico with her family. In her spare time, she likes to swim, garden, cook, and walk.